PATS FAMILY COOKBOOK VOLUME ONE

I am writing this recipe cookbook on behalf of my long-suffering wife because she is too busy to do it herself. She claims (probably rightly) that she spends most of her time looking after me (as if). I volunteered to do this without realising what a mammoth task this would be. Ho hum life's a bitch isn't it.

I am quite a keen cook myself but I have to say any culinary skill I possess I have learnt from her. I would never have dreamt in a million years I would be interested in cooking prior to the fifty odd years we have been married.

Pat's heritage is part English/German/Hungarian she especially has inherited many recipes from her German Mother and Grandmother. The contents of this book are recipes inherited and gathered from relatives, friends, and acquaintances from around the world on our many travels. We have visited around seventy countries over the years so the recipes are quite international.

I have tried to insert a little story into as many recipes as possible as I feel some cookbooks become a little impersonable just listing ingredients and method of cooking.

Well, that's about it I'll get on with the nitty gritty I hope dear reader you enjoy especially by trying the contents therein.

Bon Appetit

John Spindler

THE AUTHOR and part time cook

THE CHIEF CHEF

Pat and I very rarely have starters at home however these are a few dishes we have come across on our travels.

Prawn Cocktail

This is obviously an old favourite this is her take on it.

Ingredients

Lettuce

8oz Peeled Prawns(frozen)

Salad Cream

Tomato Ketchup

Worcester Sauce

Paprika if liked

Method

Half fill four stem glasses with shredded lettuce, fill the glasses with some prawns. Add ½ jar of salad cream, three teaspoons of tomato ketchup and a dash of Worcester sauce. Pour over prawns and sprinkle a dash of paprika if liked.

Enjoy

Smoked Salmon Parcels

I'm not a great lover of smoked salmon but Pat loves it so if that's your taste think you'll like this

Ingredients

King prawns frozen (cooked) 200g

Jar of chargrilled peppers 300g

Cream cheese 200g

Grated rind of 1/2 lemon

Pack of smoked salmon 250g

Lemon wedges

Salad leaves

Method

Chop ¾ of prawns and chargrilled peppers and blend with cream cheese and grated lemon.

Place spoonful of mix on each salmon slice and fold into a parcel.

Place on a plate and garnish with additional prawns and salad leaves.

Serve with brown bread and butter or crusty French stick.

Delicious according to Pat.

Nice glass of Pinot Grigio would help in my opinion or maybe even a Bucks Fizz.

Arme Ritter

This is a German dish that we have fairly regularly normally with leftover bread or especially French stick. It can be an extra to lunch or just a snack. It literally means Poor Knight and I guess it's a posh substitute for the Knight when he can't get anything too grand as becomes his status

Ingredients

Leftover bread or French stick

Butter softened

Sugar

Method

Cut rolls in half or French Bread into pieces about 10cm wide. Cut slice horizontally in half.

Spread soften butter thinly onto cut surface. Fry in a pan over medium to low heat until almost golden brown. Turn over and put a little butter on the other side and fry until golden brown.

Remove from pan and sprinkle with sugar.

And that's it a very simple dish but one we both love especially after lunch but you can have it morning noon and night and it uses up excess breads.

Enjoy

Kartoffelpuffer

Another German snacky type meal literally Potato Pancakes.

Both Pat and I really like these but an unusual combination for English people I suspect.

Ingredients

For two people

2-3 large peeled potatoes

One egg

Approx. two tablespoons plain flour

Half an onion finely grated

Method

Grate potato coarsely into a bowl. Add finely grated onion (not too much). Add egg and flour mix well.

Heat a little oil in a pan, when hot add a large spoonful or two of mixture and press down with back of spoon to make a this layer. Continue to fry until golden and crispy. Turn over and cook the other side. Sprinkle with sugar and gobble up.

You may find the mixture of potato and sugar unusual but trust me its very good.

Another meal as an extra to lunch or whenever you feel like a snack that's a bit different.

Give it a go I dare you.

Gurken Salat

This is a German side dish which is especially good with fish in my opinion. It literally means cucumber salad.

Ingredients

Whole cucumber peeled and thinly sliced

Salt

Half a small onion

2-3 tablespoons wine vinegar (Pat uses German white vinegar not malt)

Two teaspoons sugar

Sour cream or Greek yoghurt

Chopped dill

Method

Mix all ingredients leave to mingle and check to taste before serving

Smoky Bacon and Split Pea Soup

This is a very tasty and wholesome soup

Ingredients

225g yellow split peas soaked

225g smoked bacon chopped

One onion chopped

One large carrot chopped

Two bay leaves

1.2 litres vegetable stock

3 tbsp fresh parsley chopped

Salt and pepper

Method

Drain and rinse peas and place in a large pan

Add all other ingredients except parsley.

Bring to the boil and continue boiling for about 10 minutes then simmer for about 45 minutes under reduced heat or until peas are tender. Blend soup in a food processor until smooth.

Return to pan and garnish with chopped parsley.

We have a glut of flatleaf parsley growing in our garden it is a very useful addition to many recipes a herb my wife really adores.

Pat's leek and potato soup

Lovely soup with simple ingredients scrumptious

Ingredients

2 leeks chopped

2-3 large potatoes cubed

2 large onions chopped

2 vegetable stock cubes

1 ½ pints water

Method

Fry onions and potatoes until soft. Add rest of ingredients and bring to a boil. Then simmer for 30 minutes.

Using a hand held mixer reduce to a smooth consistency.

Add further seasoning if required.

It's that easy, lovely tasty soup for lunch or whenever you fancy.

Prawns provencal

A nice and tasty lunch or main

Ingredients

Pack of raw frozen king prawns

One onion chopped

Three cloves of garlic grated

Tin of chopped tomatoes

Tomato puree

Splash of white wine

Fresh parsley or dill finely chopped

Boiled rice

Method

Lightly fry prawns until pink only 1-2 minutes each side don't over cook as they will become chewy then set aside.

Fry onion until soft then add garlic and fry for one minute

Pour in wine and stir to loosen any debris

Add puree and stir and fry

Add tomatoes and continue cooking

Add prawns and heat through don't overcook

Dish up boiled rice we use rice cooker it works well

Season if necessary

Add provencal sauce to dish and garnish with parsley or dill

Dried tarragon is a good alternative

A glass of white wine is a must

Cheers

Lasagna

Pats take on the classic Italian dish-lovely

Ingredients

8 lasagne sheets

2 tablespoons oil

1 onion finely chopped

1 carrot finely chopped

1 garlic clove crushed

350g pork or beef mince

1 can chopped tomatoes

2 tablespoons tomato puree

4 tablespoons red wine

1 teaspoon dried oregano

1 bay leaf

Bechamel sauce:

500ml milk

Few slice raw onion

1 bay leaf

40g butter

40g flour

30g cheese grated

1 tablespoon parmesan cheese grated

Method

Cook lasagne sheets in boiled salted water with 1 tablespoon oil drain on kitchen paper.

Fry the onion, carrot and garlic in remaining oil for about 5 minutes. Stir in mince and cook for about 5 minutes stirring. Add tomatoes, puree, wine, seasoning, oregano and bay leaf. Cover and simmer for around 40 minutes stirring occasionally.

To make bechamel sauce place the milk in a pan with onion and bay leaf bring slowly to the boil and leave to cool. Melt the butter in a pan stir in the flour and cook for one minute. Strain the infused milk and gradually add to the roux stirring continuously until boiling. Simmer for 2 minutes then taste and adjust seasoning.

Place lasagne in a lightly greased ovenproof dish about 5cm deep. Spread a layer of meat and continue layering with meat sauce finishing with the bechamel sauce. Alternatively use a layer of bechamel with each meat layer.

Sprinkle with Cheddar and Parmesan cheese and cook at 180C fan for 25 minutes until golden brown and bubbling.

Wunderbar a glass or two of vino is a must as an accompaniment.

Enjoy

Aperitifs a few ideas

I personally am quite happy with a glass of white wine

Pinot Grigio is a popular one along with Sauvignon Blanc Chenin Blanc or white Rioja

If you want to go up market Chablis is the one for me

Pat doesn't like Chardonnay but I would be quite happy with it

What she really like is a good old Gin and Tonic as well Champagne but not Prosecco there's a story to that I'll tell you about another time…

There is a very wide range of Gin these days as well as flavoured ones

They are all fine by me. Another one I like but don't have much these days is Pernod with ice and water very refreshing.

Red Wine favs-Me-Rioja, Chianti, Cabernet Sauvignon

Pat-Pinot Noire, Cote de Rhone, Rioja

Pasta with bacon

This recipe is for two people but obviously it can for more just adjust the ingredient amounts. It's pretty simple and tastes great.

Ingredients

150g penne pasta

1 onion finely chopped

2 rashers bacon chopped

2 cloves garlic chopped

Tin of chopped tomatoes

½ tsp dried basil

½ tsp dried oregano

Salt and pepper

Pinch of sugar

Fresh basil leaves as garnish

Grated cheese

Method

Fry onion in a little oil until starting to soften. Add bacon and fry gently for a few minutes. Add chopped garlic and stir well. Then add tomatoes oregano and basil. Bring to boil and then simmer for about 15-20 minutes.

Boil pasta until al dente. Drain and add to sauce, tossing around well. Sauce should not be too wet. Top with fresh basil leaves and grated cheese.

A chopped chilli can be added if liked.

Pasta with bacon, tomatoes and herbs

Pretty simple dish but actually very tasty

Ingredients

For two people

150g pasta pat used penne but any will do

1 onion finely chopped

2 rashers bacon chopped

2 cloves garlic chopped

½ a pepper chopped

Tin of chopped tomatoes

½ tsp dried basil

½ tsp dried oregano

Salt and pepper

Pinch sugar

Method

Fry onion in a little oil until starting to soften. Add bacon and pepper and fry gently. Add chopped garlic and stir well. Then add tomatoes and herbs. Bring to the boil and then simmer for 15-20 minutes.

Meanwhile boil pasta until al dente. Drain and add to sauce tossing around well9sauce should not be too wet). Top with fresh basil leaves and grated cheese.

A chopped chili could be added if liked.

There we are dead simple and pretty cheap tastes great had it many times. A nice glass of chianti a must

Chicken Fricasee

Nice to do with leftover roast chicken easy and tasty.

This is a great and easy way to use up leftover roast chicken.

Ingredients

8oz long grain rice

8 oz onions

4 oz butter

12 oz leftover roast chicken

Salt and pepper

12oz mixed cooked vegtables

1 level teaspoon curry powder

2 tablespoons soy sauce

One egg

Method

Cook rice in boiling salted waster for about 12minutes or use a rice cooker. Turn into a sieve and rinse in cold water until clean leaving to drain. Cut oinions in rings and fryin half butter in a large pan or wok. Cook for about 20 minutes over medium heat brtowning very slowly. Add rest of butter, rice, mixed vegtables, salt and pepper, curry powder and soy sauce. Blend well over the heat until piping hot. Add chicken to the wok and mix in well to warm meat through. Dish up onto plates.

Garnish with one egg thin omlette like a pancake cutting into thin strips and make a lattice pattern on top of plated dishes.

And that's it a simple dish but very tasty.

PAELLA

This is my take on the classic spanish dish. One of my creations I cook as well folks.

There are many recipes for Paella this is just my idea.

Ingredients

A nice hearty meal or a quick lunch time snack the choice is yours

Ingredients

For 4 people

50g bacon chopped

1 onion chopped

I garlic clove crushed

250g green lentils

400g can chopped tomatoes

250g Mattesons cooked spicy sausage

750g water

1 teaspoon paprika

Salt and pepper to taste

Method

Fry the bacon in a large pan add onion and saute until softened. Add garlic to mixure and continue to saute. Add remaining ingredients after washing lentils. Bring to the boil, cover and simmer 35-40 minutes.

That's is a simple and satisfying meal it doesn't need anything else except the compulsory glass of vino.

Pat's Lamb Pasties

Excellent pasties to use leftover roast lamb

Ingredients

200g plain flour

Pinch of salt

100g butter

Water to mix

175g cooked lamb approx. chopped in processor but if you have more use it up just make more pasties adjusting measures

1 onion finely chopped

50g cooked peas

100g boiled potatoes chopped

Salt and ground pepper

5g dried mint

Beaten egg for glazing

Method

Sieve flour with a pinch of salt into a bowl. Add butter and rub in until mixture looks like breadcrumbs. Add cold water to make a pliable dough and knead lightly until smooth. Wrap in foil and chill for 30 minutes.

Mix together lamb, onion, peas, potatoes, salt and pepper to taste then add mint.

Roll out pastry on a floured surface and cut into circles 18cm in diameter. Divide meat mixture in the centre of each. Damp the pastry edges and join together at the top to form a pasty. Press together and crimp the edge. Place on a dampened baking sheet and brush with beaten egg. Cook in hot oven at 200c fan for 15 minutes then reduce to 160c fan for further 15 minutes until well browned.

Serve with vegetable of your choice delicious.

One of mine hope you like it

Ingredients

For two people

One large breast of chicken cut into bite size chunks

Small can of pineapple rings in juice cut into chunks

Oil (not olive)

One large onion cut into chunks

One red pepper chopped

Cornflour

2 spring onions

Two garlic cloves sliced

Fresh root ginger grated (leave peel on)

Tbsp dark soy

2 tbsp white wine vinegar

2 tbsp light brown sugar

2 tbsp tomato ketchup

Chili flakes

Chinese vegetable e.g. pak choi chopped

Boiled rice

Method

Heat oil in wok fry chicken doused lightly in cornflour until golden brown set aside

Fry onion and pepper adding more oil if necessary until lightly browned set aside with chicken

Put garlic, ginger, soy, vinegar, sugar, ketchup and chilli in a bowl adding juice from pineapple can and mix well

Stir fry pak choi until wilted return chicken and cooked onion and pepper to wok continue cooking and add sauce mix along with pineapple chunks. Stir fry for about 10 minutes until chicken is cooked through.

Add a little cornflour mixed with water in a cup to thicken the sauce.

Garnish with spring onions sliced at an angle

Plate up with freshly cooked rice (I use a rice cooker)

Have a good slurp of white wine while doing this to keep you well oiled

That's it I'm sure you'll enjoy this I know we do.

Bon appetite

Special occasion Planner

Chicken a la iris

Iris is a German relative of Pats. This is a lovely way to cook chicken breast very succulent.

Ingredients

2 chicken breasts butterflied then covered in cling film and flattened

Butter for frying

3 garlic cloves crushed

Flour

2 eggs

50g parmesan cheese

For the sauce

170ml chicken stock

3 garlic cloves crushed

Juice of ½ lime

Chopped parsley

Butter

Method

Flour chicken breasts both sides.

Mix together beaten eggs garlic and parmesan cheese.

Dip chicken breasts in mixture and fry chicken both sides until golden. Set aside.

For the sauce mix chicken stock, garlic, lime juice and parsley. Heat together with butter. Then place chicken back in pan and heat through.

To serve spoon sauce over the cooked chicken.

Serve with potatoes and green beans.

Schmeckt Prima

Roast chicken with stuffing

Planner for a crowd

Pork sausages with messy potatoes

Pat's version of an old favourite bangers and mash. Good stuff this is.

Ingredients

For 2 people

Pack of six pork sausages any variety

Potatoes for mashing your choice of quantity

2 rashers back bacon trimmed and chopped

One medium onion chopped

Tin of baked beans

Cooking oil

Brown sauce or tomato ketchup

Milk

Butter

Method

Fry onion and bacon until crispy then set aside

Boil potatoes

Fry sausages until nicely browned and cooked through set aside and keep warm reheat bacon mix gently

Drain cooked potatoes and mash thoroughly and mix in bacon and onion add some milk and butter when mashing potatoes

Heat baked beans in micro wave or on hob.

Serve sausages and mash with baked beans then slop on plenty of brown sauce or ketchup.Yummy

Gefullte Paprikaschoten

44

Stuffed peppers one of Pat's favourites. Her Mum used to cook her this as a child. Peppers stuffed with pork mince and onion.

Ingredients

For four people

Four peppers

500g pork mince (beef could be used)

1 onion chopped

1 egg

1 slice of bread soaked in water and squeezed dry

2 tins tomato soup or homemade soup

Salt and pepper

Method

Carefully cut round the stalk 0f the peppers and remove. Take all seeds out plus any loose pieces inside the peppers. Rinse out thoroughly.

Mix mince, onion, egg and bread which needs breaking into small pieces. Place into a large bowl. Add salt and pepper to taste. Mix well with a fork until well combined. Using a teaspoon fill peppers with meat mixture. Press down inside the peppers with fingers.

Place peppers into a saucepan to fit fairly snugly. Add 2 tin tomato soup rinsing each tin with some water and add to saucepan. The tops may poke out a little.

Bring to the boil, then simmer gently for 45 minutes. Turn peppers onto their sides after about 20 minutes so they cook evenly. Serve with crushed boiled potatoes and generous helping of the sauce.

Magnifique, keep some sauce for a soup the next day for lunch.

Berliner Boulette

Berlin style meatballs

One of Pats favourites which surprises me as it is a pretty straightforward
has influe

Ingredients

500g Pork mince

One chopped onion

One egg beaten

Breadcrumbs or one slice of bread soaked then squeezed

Salt and pepper

Potatoes boiled and mashed with milk and butter

Green beans or frozen peas boiled

Method

Mix all ingredients together with a fork or wooden spoon season well

Shape into balls and then flatten with hand

Fry until browned on both sides and cooked through and keep warm

Boil potatoes and mash adding milk and butter

Boil veg

Plate up and that's it a simple dish we like plenty of brown sauce splashed on top of meat and potatoes

Enjoy

Kohlrouladen

Stuffed cabbage leaves

Not a straightforward recipe but the end result is worth it.

Ingredients

Savoy cabbage if ordinary cabbage choose large leaves

Pork mince or beef if preferred

1 onion finely chopped

1 egg

Salt and pepper

1 chicken stock cube

A little cornflour

Method

Bring a large saucepan of water to the boil, then simmer.

Peel off outer leaves of cabbage without breaking them. Put them into water and simmer until starting to bend. Not long needed probably around five minutes. Remove from water and rinse under cold water. Then drain on a colander. Continue with more leaves, you could put whole cabbage in if you prefer then peel off softened outer leaves then put the rest of the cabbage into the water and continue until you have enough at least ten leaves.

Mix together meat, bread, egg, salt and pepper and onion. Make sure it is nicely combined.

Lay leaves on a board and carefully shave off the thickest part of the leaf leaving it intake and easy to roll up using a sharp knife or serrated one.

Place a tablespoon or a little more of the meat mixture at the stalk end of the leaves, roll up and cover meat then fold in sides and roll again so that the seam is at the bottom. Continue until all the meat mixture is used up. Place on a plate. Once completed heat a little oil in a frying pan and brown both sides. Single layer only. Carefully remove and place in a ovenproof dish close together and large enough to have them in a single layer.

Then add approximately ½ pint of water and one chicken stock cube into an empty sauce pan. Bring to the boil and pour over cabbage rolls. About half way up the rolls do not cover. Cover with foil and cook at 170c fan assisted for one hour.

Once cooked remove cabbage rolls and thicken sauce with a little cornflour and add a grating of nutmeg. Check seasoning. Pour over cabbage rolls and serve with mashed potatoes and a your choice of vegetable.

Well that's it a bit intricate Pat does it no sweat no chance of me trying it though. I would add it tastes great especially with a nice glass of red.

Enjoy

An old English favourite Pat prefers to cook this with pork mince but beef or lamb can be used.

Ingredients

For 4 people

500g pork mince

Tin of chopped tomatoes

Tomato puree

Worcester sauce

One large onion chopped

½ grated peeled carrot

Beef stock pot

Bisto powder for thickening

Potatoes for mashing

Grated cheddar cheese

Milk

Method

Add onion to largish pot and gently soften but not brown frying in oil and butter mix. Add mince to pot and brown on higher heat until no pink meat left. Add tomato puree and tin tomatoes and gently bring to boil. Add Worcester sauce and stock pot and some water and continue to boil. Turn down heat and simmer gently uncovered for about 20 minutes. Add bisto powder and stir constantly until sauce thickens. Allow mixture to cool.

In the meantime peel and boil potatoes, drain and mash when properly cooked about 10-15 minutes. Add some milk and stir into mash to remove any lumps.

Pour sauce into oblong baking dish and add mashed potatoes smoothing out with a fork to make even covering. Top with grated cheese to make a good finish. Bake at 170c fan oven for about 20 minutes until surface it nicely browned.

Serve with green vegetable frozen peas go well.

As I mentioned above pat cooks this with pork mince as she is not keen on beef or lamb mince but either are acceptable depends on your taste.

Very moreish.

Of course a nice glass of vino is a must.

Chilli con carne

A nice warming dish for supper

Ingredients

500gr pork or beef mince (Pat uses pork)

One large red pepper

Two onions chopped

Tin of chopped tomatoes

Tomato puree

Chilli powder or flakes

Tin red kidney beans preferably in chilli sauce

Teaspoon marjoram powder

Beef stock pot

Two teaspoons paprika

Rice for boiling

3 cloves garlic crushed

Method

Gently fry onions in large pot until softish add pepper and do the same. Add garlic and fry gently for a minute or two. Add mince turn up heat and brown until no red meat showing.

Add tomato puree and cook briefly then add tin tomatoes and warm through. Add chilli flakes or powder with marjoram and paprika then continue cooking. Melt stock pot in 200-300 ml of boiling water and add to mixture. Simmer on hob for about 30-40 minutes adding kidney beans 10 minutes before completion.

I always think dishes like chilli are best left for flavours to mingle then re heated you can even freeze it for a later date.

Boil some rice for serving and that's it job done.

Recipe Notes

Leftover Beef with onions

Great way to use up leftover roast beef

This is a straightforward but delicious way to use leftovers from the Sunday roast. If you have leftover veg such as roast potatoes parsnips brussels etc turn it into bubble and squeak and save some Yorkshire pud too. Delicious.

Ingredients

Serves 2-4 people

Leftover roast beef thinly sliced

1 large onion thinly sliced

Cheddar cheese grated

Leftover gravy or bisto if none available to moisten beef

Method

Lay beef on bottom of oven proof dish. Moisten with a little gravy.

Fry onion in a little oil and butter until golden and softened.

Spread onion over beef.

Top with grated cheddar.

Bake at 170C fan assisted for 20-30 minutes until cheese is browned.

Serve with potatoes and a vegetable or as is mentioned above bubble and squeak from leftover veg (fried leftovers).

And don't forget some Yorkshires (see roast beef recipe for this)

Delicious

Summer Menu

Beef Rouladen

A German dish literally stuffed beef a lovely dish

Ingredients

For four people

Four thinly sliced beef stakes

Dijon mustard

Four rashers back bacon trimmed

One finely chopped onion

Cornflour

Potatoes

Green beans

Method

Flatten steaks to tenderise. Then spread each one with a thin layer of mustard. Place a rasher of bacon on each steak and a small pile of chopped onion. Roll steaks and fasten with cocktail sticks. Fry the rolled steaks to brown. When completed place in a deep baking tray and fill with water until halfway up rolled steaks. Cover with foil and bake at 170c fan for about one hour. Check for tenderness and if necessary bake a little longer. Remove steaks and thicken sauce with a little cornflour.

Boil some potatoes and crush when boiled adding a little butter.

Boile green beans to serve.

This is a delicious recipe and of would be even better with a nice glass of red wine!

Enjoy

Winter Menu

Hungarian Goulash

Pat prefers to cook this dish with pork although beef can be used.

A nice dish with a bit of oomph of spicy Hungarian paprika.

Ingredients

400-500g braising steak or pork leg/loin cut into chunks

2-3 onions finely chopped

1-2 garlic cloves chopped

Tin of chopped tomatoes

1 tblsp tomato puree

1 pepper cut into squares

1 tblsp paprika

1 tsp hot paprika

Sour cream or Greek yoghurt

Method

Fry onions gently until softened then add meat a few pieces at a time until everything is well mixed. Add garlic, stir in then add tomatoes, tomato puree and add a little water to just cover the meat. Add pepper and paprika and stir well. Add salt to taste. Cover and cook in oven 160c fan assisted or reg 4 for approx. one hour(pork) or 2 hours (beef).

Check a couple of times during cooking and add a little more water if required.

Add a dollop of sour cream on top.

Serve with potatoes and green vegetables.

As a little aside if you add sauerkraut with a little extra water 30 minutes before the end of cooking the goulash it becomes Szegediner Goulash another Hungarian variation. Sauerkraut is not everybodies cup of tea but Pat and I love it the choice is yours.

Oven Baked Salmon and Peas

Salmon is not my favourite food so I tend to either cover it with sweet chilli sauce or make a sauce vierge (mix capers, spring onions, halved small tomatoes, lemon juice, tarragon and olive oil) serve as a relish uncooked.

For two people

Ingredients

2 salmon filets

A little butter

Salt and pepper to taste

4 slices of lemon

Chopped parsley or dill

Method

Line oven dish with parchment paper

Place Salmon on top. Sprinkle with salt and pepper and lay 2 slices of lemon on each filet. Cover with foil and bake for about 20 minutes 170c fan assisted.

Remove from oven once cooked.

Remove the lemon and garnish with chopped parsley or dill.

Serve with potatoes boiled/ mashed/ or fried. Boil some garden peas and voila you are ready to eat.

Nice glass of white wine. Job done.

Kasekuchen

German cheesecake

Cake Notes

Ingredients

500g quark

200g cream cheese

100g sugar

4 eggs

Grated rind 1-2 lemons

75g sultanas

Butter

Method

Grease a leak proof tin or pyrex dish (approx. 24cm x 6cm deep) with butter.

Mix cheese and quark together. Then add sugar, lemon rind and eggs mix well.

Add 75g sultanas

Pour into dish and bake 45-50 minutes at 160 degrees fan assisted oven.

This was one of Pats mums favourites it was a regular when we went round her parents house. Recommended.

Pineapple upside down cake

An unusual cake but very tasty with a different look about it.

Ingredients

50g soft brown sugar

50g softened butter beaten with above

1 tin pineapple rings

Glace cherries

100g softened butter

100g sugar

100g self raising flour

1 tsp baking powder

2 eggs

2 tbsps pineapple juice or milk

Method

Place butter and sugar mix into bottom of 8 inch/20cm sandwich tin

Place well drained pineapple rings on top with cherry placed in centre of each ring.

Mix together sponge mixture in stand mixer or electric whisk. Spread evenly over pineapple. Level off. Bake 30-35 minutes 160 degrees fan assisted oven until skewer comes out clean.

Lovely cake and relatively easy to bake and eat especially eat.

Torten Boden

This a recipe for a flan case which can be used to fill with fruit especially strawberries apricots plums or peaches. If doing so a gelatine should be used.

Ingredients

125gr sugar

125gr butter

2 eggs

125gr cornflour and plain flour mixed half and half

Grated lemon rind

Level teaspoon baking powder add to flour mixture

Method

Beat sugar, butter and lemon rind until creamy. Then add one egg and half flour mixture. Then add the other egg and rest of flour.

Beat a little, not too much as it shouldn't be an easily spreadable mixture.

Spread over bottom of greased large circular cake tin.

Bake 160 degrees Centigrade fan assisted or regolo 5 gas for 55-60 minutes.

Poke with skewer to test if done.

Turn out fill with fruit and pour over gelatine or tortenguss.

This is a fantastic looking and tasting flan believe me I've had it loads of times with all different fruits a bit of whipped cream helps.

A nice easy recipe but outcome is some yummy buns that don't last long from hungry hands.

Ingredients

200g self raising flour

100g butter

75g sugar

100g mixed dried fruit

I egg beaten

Milk to mix

Method

Sift flour and rub in flour finely. Then add sugar and mixed fruit.

Mix to very stiff batter with egg and milk.

Place spoonfuls of mixture in rough rocky shapes on a greased baking tray allowing room for expansion on tray.

Bake for 20 minutes at 160c in fan assisted oven.

Remove and cool a little on rack then consume with a nice cuppa.

Delicious

These are easy to make even I can do it and I'm no baker.

Enjoy

Quick Scones

Easy scone recipe just add jam and butter or cream loverly

Ingredients

225g self raising flour

1 tsp baking powder

50g butter

25g sugar

1 egg beaten

Milk added to egg to make up to 125ml

Method

Rub in method mix flour and baking powder with butter and sugar (muscovite sugar and 1 tblsp golden syrup can be added to egg mixture if preferred) then mix with milk to make 125ml. save one tablespoon for brushing scone tops.

Cut out to 1.25 cm and cut brush tops with milk mixture when placing in a baking tray.

Bake for 10 minutes at 200c fan assisted.

And voila that's it simple and splendid just add jam/cream/butter or eat on their own.

Bon appetite !

Pat's Mince Pies

You'll love these they disappear at a rate of knots at christmas

Ingredients

120 oz plain flour

4oz icing or caster sugar

9oz butter cut into small pieces

Finely grated rind and juice of one large lemon

milk

2 jars mincemeat (400gr)

Method

Make pastry quickly mixing ingredients and chill 30 minutes before use. Cut into baking tray and fill with mincemeat. Bake 20-25 minutes at 180c fan after brushing tops with milk should make 36 pies.

Lovely tasting pies.

Carrot cake

This'll fill a hole.

Ingredients

12 oz grated carrots

4 eggs

8oz brown sugar

6 fl oz oil

8oz wholemeal self raising flour

2 teaspoons ground cinnamon

4oz desicated coconut

4oz raisins

Grated orange rind

Method

Grease an 8 inch(20cm) square tin. Whisk eggs and sugar togetrher until thick and creamy. Add oil slowly but whisking.Add all other ingredients spoon into tin. Level the top and bake 50-60 minutes at 160c fan assisted until firm to the touch and golden brown.

Unusual to bake cake with oil rather than butter but tastes great. You can top with roasted almonds or even add icing but basic cake is excellent.

Carrot cake with cream topping

Pat cooked this as a birthday cake for our granddaughter it's yummy

Cook two cakes as per previous carrot cake recipe round or oblong.

Ingredients for cream topping

50g butter room temp

25g icing sugar

250g full fat cream cheese room temp

3 drops vanilla extract

Method

Mix all ingredients using hand or electric whisk until smooth and thoroughly blended.

Spread half onto one cake. Place other on top. Make swirl pattern on top.

Decorate with walnuts or other bought decorations.

Wunderbar

Party time enjoy

Pats iced buns

Very nice and light, if you wish to freeze them do so uniced.

You can make dough. Put into a bowl, cover and leave overnight in fridge. Continue next day.

Ingredients

500g strong plain flour

7g sachet yeast

50g sugar

50g unsalted butter softened

One egg beaten

140ml water and 160ml milk mixed together

Method

Mix ingredients all together in stand mixer or bread machine.

Knead 10minutes in stand mixer if using.

Cover and leave to prove until doubled in size 1 ½-2 hours.

Double line large baking sheet/tin with parchment paper.

Punch air out of dough on floured board. Cut into twelve pieces.

Roll each piece into a smooth round ball with hands then between both hands forming a sausage shape. Dusting hands first with flour.

8-10cm long 3cm wide

Transfer to baking sheet leaving 2cm between buns.

Cover with lightly oiled clingfilm and leave to prove for 30 minutes-1 hour. Could be longer if cooler temperature.

Heat oven 190c fan (gas 7).

Remove clingfilm and bake approx 10-12 minutes until golden.

Remove and leave on wire rack to cool completely.

Meanwhile mix 1560g iciing sugar with a little water to make a thick coating.

Add a few drops of almond essence or lemon rind to taste.

Spread mixture over buns once they are cold.

That's it enjoy.

These buns are delicious especially when eaten fresh.

As I said at the beginning they are very light and are definitely moreish.

Nice cuppa or a coffee are the best accompanimant.

Lemon Yoghurt Drizzle Cake

Ingredients

250g softened unsalted butter

275g sugar

275g self raising flour

4 eggs

Grated rind of 2 lemons

3 tablespoons lemon juice

100g greek yoghurt

Method

Beat the butter and sugar until light and fluffy. Add lemon rind and one egg at a time beating well in between. Fold in flour, lemon juice and yoghurt.

Bake in lined loaf tin 30cm x 11cm approx or 8-9 inch round tin for 40-50 minutes at 160c. cook until skwer comes out clean.

Prick all over with skewer. Pour over the following- grated rind and four tablespoons lemon juice plus 150g icing sugar mixed together.

Leave to cool.

That's it all done delicious and crumtious cake.

Enjoy

CHOCOLATE CHIP COOKIES

These biscuits are lovely don't leave them laying around they tend to disappear rapido.

Ingredients

120g unsalted butter softened

75g light brown sugar

75g granulated sugar

½ packet vanill;a sugar or I teasp vanilla essence

1 medium egg

180g plain flour

½ teasp bicarb of soda

100g chocolate chips

¼ teasp salt

Method

Heat oven 160c fan/reg 4

Line 2 trays with parchment paper

Beat butter and sugar together until light and fluffy. Add egg and beat into butter mixture. Mix together flour, bicarb, choc chips and salt. Add to butter and sugar mix. Stir don't beat. Mix until combined.

Roll into balls using approx 1 tablespoon for each.

Placr 5 on each tray.

Bake 10-12 minutes until edges are firm but middle still soft. Leave to cool on paper. Once cool place on a rack to cool further.

That's it georgeous enjoy.

Ginger Biscuits

Nice and tasty ginger biscuits one of my favourite snacks

Ingredients

100g unsalted butter

75g light brown soft sugar

1 tbsp fresh ginger grated finely

100g golden syrup

250g self raising flour

1½ tbsp ground ginger

1 tsp bicarb of soda

1 small egg yolk beaten

Method

Heat oven 170c fan/reg 5

Line 2 trays with baking parchment

In a saucepan over low heat melt butter, sugar, fresh ginger and syrup then leave to cool.

Mix flour, ground ginger and bicarb together in a bowl with wooder spoon.

Gradually stir in the cooled sugar mixture and egg yolk then knead to make a dough.

Roll dough into 20g balls walnut size and put on baking trays with 3cm between each to allow for spreading

Bake 8-10 minutes until golden drown. Leave in trays to cool for a minute or two then transfer to a cooling rack to cool completely.

All done great with a cup of tea or coffee

Enjoy

Pats Jammy Biscuits

Ingredients

200g self raising flour

100g caster sugar

100g butter

1 egg lightly beaten

1+ tbsp strawberry jam

Method

Heat oven 170c fan/ reg 5

Rub butter flour and sugar together until it looks like fine breadcrumbs. Or use processor. Add enough egg to bring mixture together to form a stiff dough.

Flour hands and shape dough into a tube about 5cm diameter. Cut into 2cm thick slices and place on a large baking sheet. Space out well.

Make a small dent in middle of each slice with end of wooden spoon and drop a tsp of jam in centre. Bake for 10-15 minutes until slightly risen and just golden.

Cool on a wire rack and you're done.

Nice with a cup of coffee or tea.

Pain de Campagne

A lovely bread for lunch with cheese or ham

Ingredients

400g strong white flour

100g rye flour

2 teaspoons salt

30g yeast/ 2 teaspoons (1 packet)

50g butter softened

2 teaspoons sugar

300 ml water

Method

Mix all together and leave for 2 hours. Shape dough into a ball, slightly flatten and dust with flour. Using a knife mark out a square shape on top of dough. Leave to rise for one hour

Preheat oven 190 degrees fan oven or reg 7

Bake 30 minutes until golden brown.

Transfer to wire rack to cool.

ENJOY

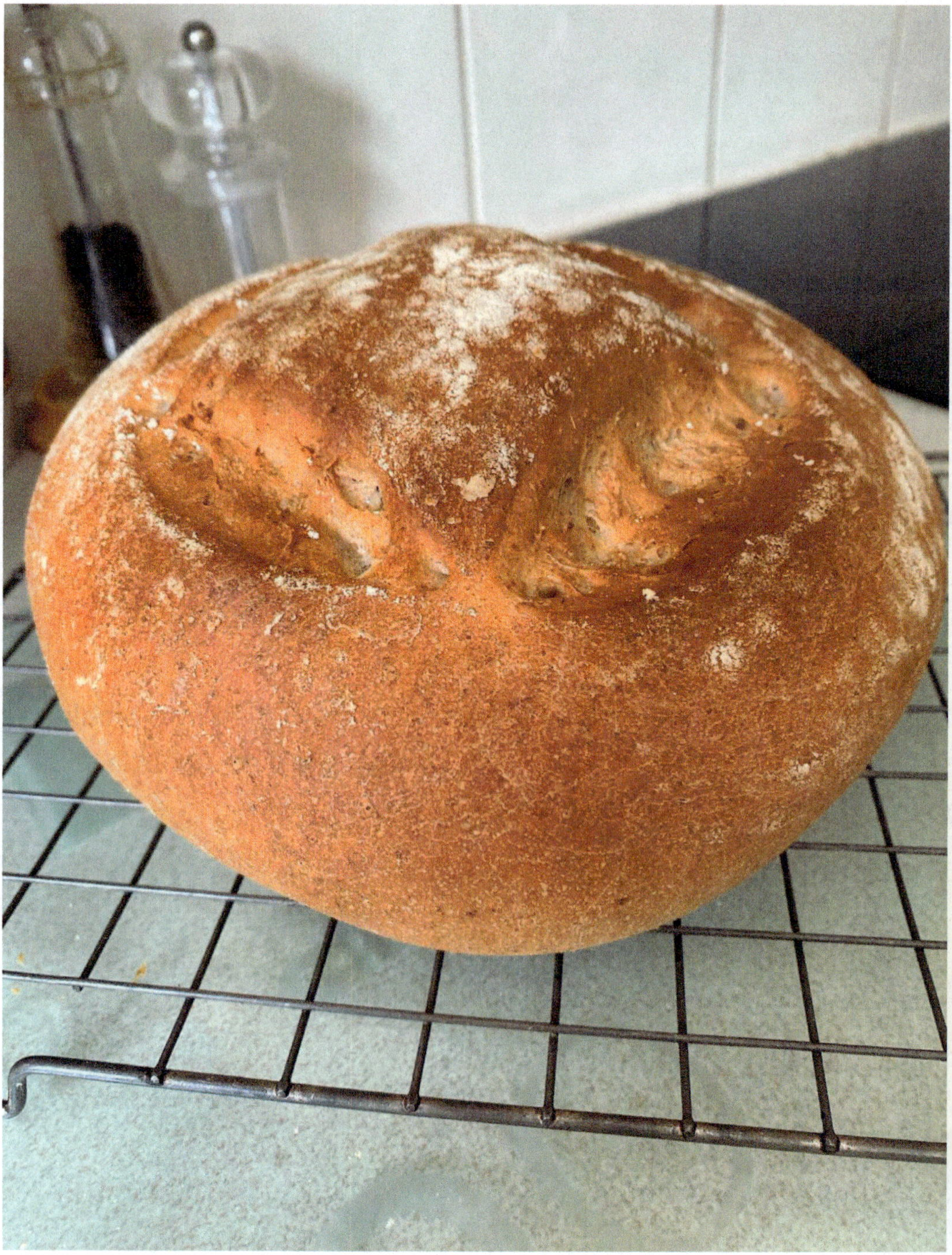

Oatmeal raisin cookies

Ingredients

240g raisins

225g plain flour

½ tsp salt

½ tsp baking powder

1 tsp cinnamon

250g unsalted butter room temp

220g brown sugar

220g white sugar

2 large eggs

300g rolled oats

Method

Heat oven 160c fan middle and low rack leave 4inches between

Soak raisins in boiling water for 10minutes. Then drain and pat dry.

Sift dry flour salt cinnamon and baking powder mixed

Cream butter and sugar having beaten butter then add sugar 2-3 minutes.

Add eggs one at a time until incorporated

Mix in flour with wooden spoon

Stir in oats abnd raisins needs effoirt as dough gets stiff

Form 4 cm balls 18 in total place on baking sheet 10cm apart. Can use ice cream scoop for this. Press lightly to form a thick disc shape

Bake for 11 minutes. Swap trays over and bake for 11-14 minutes until golden on the edge but light golden in the middle.

Cool for 5 minutes on tray. Transfer to rack and cool 30 minutes before serving

Although a bit fiddly well worth the effort.

That's it folks hope you enjoy some of Pat's recipes I will be back with volume two later

Bon appetite and Good Health!

Index

Beef

Beef Rouladen 58

Leftover Beef with Onions 56

Biscuits

Chocolate chip Cookies 83

Ginger Biscuits 85

Jammy Biscuits 87

Oatmeal Raisin Cookies 91

Bread

Arme Ritter 6

Pain de Campagne 89

Cakes

Carrot Cake 74

Carrot Cake withg Cream Topping 76

Iced Buns 78

Kasekuchen 64

Lemon Yoghurt Drizzle Cake 81

Mince Pies 72

Pineapple Upside Down Cake 66

Quick Scones 70

Rock Buns 68

Torten Boden 67

Chicken

Chicken a la Iris 39

Chicken a la Patricia 25

Chicken Fricasee 23

Roast Chicken 41

Sweet and Sour Chicken 36

Lamb

Lamb Pasties 34

Pasta

Lasagna 15

Pasta with Bacon 19

Pasta with Bacon Tomatoes and Herbs 21

Pork

Berliner Boulette 46

Chilli Con Carne 54

Hungarian Goulash 60

Kohlrouladen 48

Pork Medallions with Ham and Madeira 26

Sausages with messy Potatoes 42

Shepherds Pie 51

Stuffed Peppers 44

Potato

Kartoffelpuffer 8

Leek and Potato soup 11

Prawns

Prawn Cocktail 4

Prawns Provencal 13

Pulses

Lentils with Spicy Sausage 32

Rice

Nasi Goreng 27

Paella 29

Salad

Gurken Salat 9

Salmon

Oven Baked Salmon with Peas 62

Smoked Salmon Parcels 5

Soup

Leek and Potato Soup 11

Smoky Bacon and Split Pea Soup 10

Now for volume two asta la vista baby !!